For:

I Love You,
Be Careful!

Love:

1

Dedication

J.D. I dedicate this book to my sister, Judy, for her love and support during all of my "be careful" moments in life. She shows and knows only love and is always there to tell me to be careful. And to my husband, children, grandchildren, sisters, and friends, I love you!

J.S. Thanks to my sister, Joanie, for all of the fun that we had doing this book together. She is my inspiration and makes me laugh. I love you, Joanie! And to my husband Gil, sons Jon and Nick, and my Michigan family....I love you!

C.D. To the amazing man in my life, my husband Chris, who always inspires me to do better. I love you! To my mother Shelly and my "sister" Britta...thanks for cheering me on. To my friend, Mr. Kershaw...thanks for believing in me.

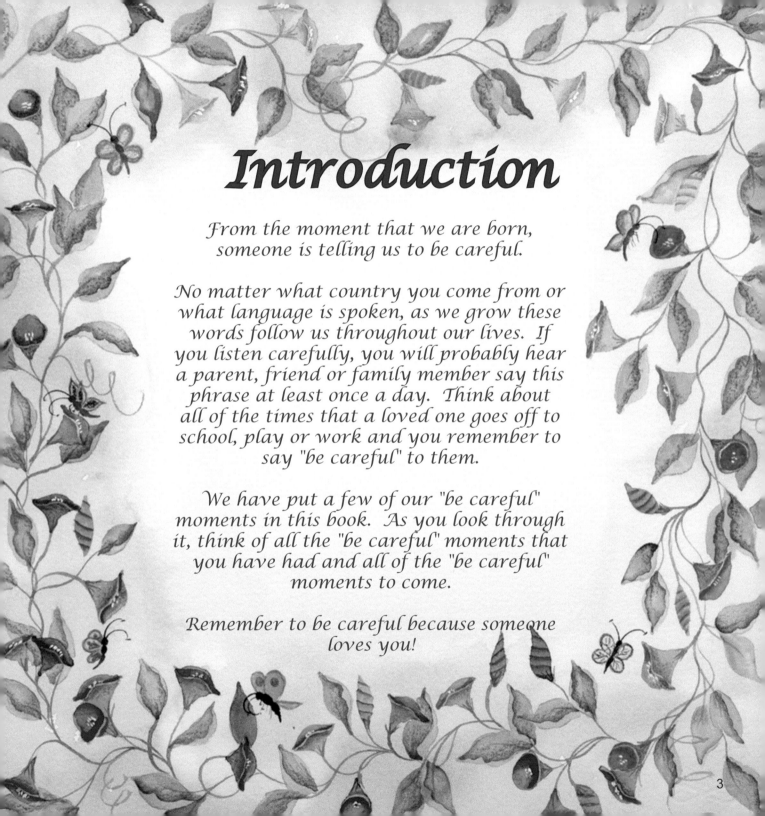

Introduction

From the moment that we are born, someone is telling us to be careful.

No matter what country you come from or what language is spoken, as we grow these words follow us throughout our lives. If you listen carefully, you will probably hear a parent, friend or family member say this phrase at least once a day. Think about all of the times that a loved one goes off to school, play or work and you remember to say "be careful" to them.

We have put a few of our "be careful" moments in this book. As you look through it, think of all the "be careful" moments that you have had and all of the "be careful" moments to come.

Remember to be careful because someone loves you!

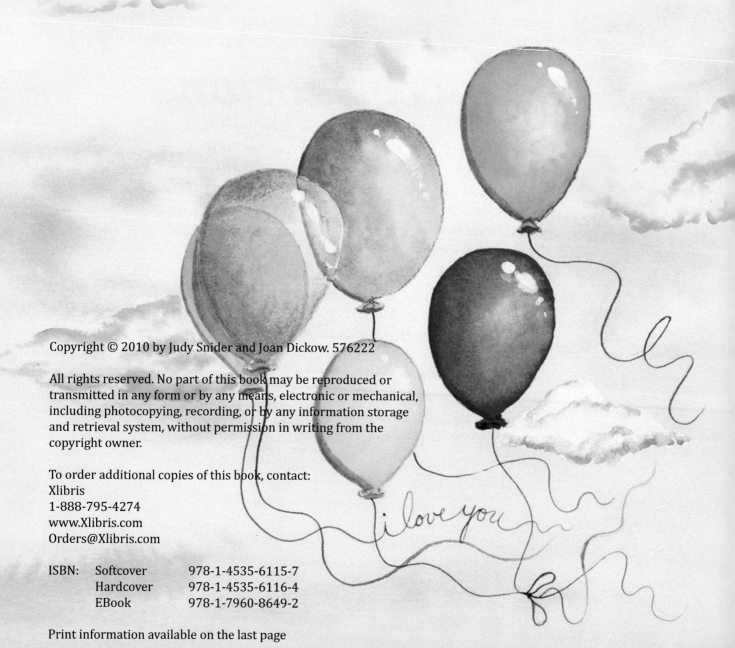

To order additional copies of this book, contact:
Xlibris
1-888-795-4274
www.Xlibris.com
Orders@Xlibris.com

ISBN: Softcover   978-1-4535-6115-7
        Hardcover   978-1-4535-6116-4
        EBook   978-1-7960-8649-2

Print information available on the last page

Rev. date: 02/03/2020

I love you... be careful!

By Judy Snider and Joan Dickow

Illustrations by Cady B. Driver

I love you...

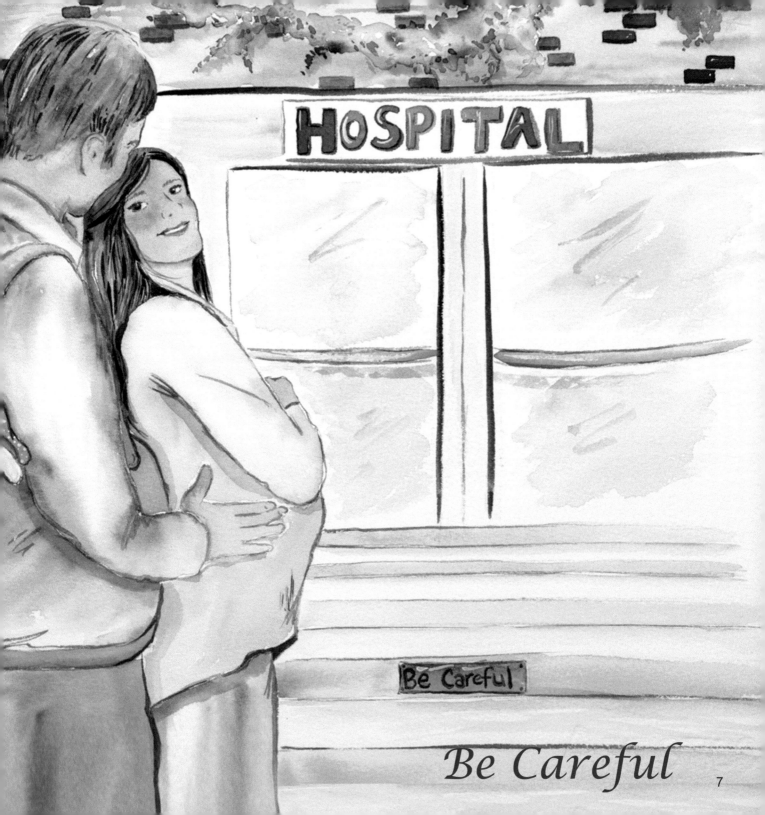

Be Careful

I love you...

Be Careful

I love you...

Be Careful

I love you...

12

Be Careful

13

I love you...

Be Careful

15

I love you...

I love you...

Be Careful

I love you...

Be Careful

I love you...

Be Careful

23

I love you...

Be Careful

I love you...

Be
Careful

I love you...

Be Careful

29

I love you...

Be Careful

I love you...

Be Careful

I love you...

Be Careful

Joan Dickow, Judy's sister, lives in Berkley, Michigan with her husband, Fred and their cat, Coffee. This is her first book and she is currently working on her second picture book, *The Porch Fairy*.

Judy Snider, Joan's sister lives in Virginia Beach, Virginia with her husband, Gil, and two silly cats. She is the author of the CWA award winning children's picture book, *Goldy's Baby Socks*, and on a team of authors of *The Sacred Purse*.

Cady Driver paints portraits and murals, teaches art and donates her work to charitable organizations. She has also illustrated *Icky, Sticky Pancake World by Patrick Wynn*. You can view more of her work online at www.ArtByCady.com or contact her at Cady@ArtByCady.com. She currently resides in Raleigh, NC with her husband and home schools her three children.

Printed in the United States
By Bookmasters